A WINNING SKILLS BOOK

You Can Handle Tough Situations!

Joy Berry

Illustrated by Bartholomew

Joy Berry Enterprises

Copyright © Joy Berry, 2022
Originally Published 2013

All rights are reserved.

No part of this book can be duplicated or used without the prior written permission of the copyright owner, except for the use of brief quotations from the book.

For inquiries or permission requests contact the publisher.

Published by Joy Berry Enterprises
www.joyberryenterprises.com

Joy Berry
Enterprises

You can handle tough situations if you know
- what tough situations are.
- the different types of tough situations.
- the various origins of tough situations.
- the six steps for handling tough situations that you create.
- the six steps for handling tough situations that you did not create.
- the things that make it easier to handle tough situations.

WHAT TOUGH SITUATIONS ARE

A tough situation is one that jeopardizes someone's happiness or well being.

A tough situation can hurt you or someone else.

DIFFERENT TYPES OF TOUGH SITUATIONS

Some tough situations cause **physical harm.**

DIFFERENT TYPES OF TOUGH SITUATIONS

Some tough situations cause **mental or emotional harm.**

THE MOST DIFFICULT SITUATION I EVER FACED WAS MY PARENTS' DIVORCE. MY DAD WANTED ME TO LIVE WITH **HIM** AND MY MOM WANTED ME TO LIVE WITH **HER**. I KNEW NO MATTER WHERE I LIVED, SOMEONE'S FEELINGS WOULD BE HURT!

DIFFERENT TYPES OF TOUGH SITUATIONS

Short-term tough situations last for a short period of time such as a hour or a day.

Long-term tough situations last for a long period of time such as several days, weeks, or months.

10 DIFFERENT TYPES OF TOUGH SITUATIONS

Whether a tough situation is short-term or long-term, it seldom disappears automatically.

In fact, a tough situation that is not handled appropriately can become worse and possibly can create additional tough situations.

To handle tough situations appropriately, it is important to determine who or what created it.

Sometimes **you** create a tough situation by breaking a natural law.

A **natural law** is a specific principle established by nature.

When you break a natural law, you often experience the negative consequences that automatically occur when the law is broken.

This puts you in a tough situation.

Sometimes **you** create a tough situation by breaking a man-made law.

A **man-made law** is a rule established by people.

When you break a man-made law, you often are forced to pay a penalty that is imposed on you by the people that enforce the law.

This puts you in a tough situation.

Common sense is good judgement that is based on simple logic and reasoning.

Sometimes you create a tough situation by disregarding your common sense and acting against it.

When you act against your common sense, you often experience the negative consequences that automatically occur when you do something that is illogical and senseless.

ORIGINS OF TOUGH SITUATIONS

Natural circumstances beyond your control are occurrences, caused by nature, that you cannot prevent or change.

ORIGINS OF TOUGH SITUATIONS

Sometimes natural circumstances beyond your control create tough situations.

Human circumstances beyond your control are occurrences, caused by other people, that you cannot prevent or change.

Sometimes human circumstances beyond your control can create tough situations.

SIX STEPS FOR HANDLING TOUGH SITUATIONS YOU CREATE

Here are six steps for handling tough situations that **you** create:

Step 1: Face it.

Admit that you are experiencing a tough situation. Do not pretend that everything is OK.

Step 2: Accept it.

Accept this fact: The tough situation is not going to go away automatically. Realize that you are going to have to put time and effort into resolving it.

Step 3: Think about it.

Find out the answers to these questions:
- What did I do to create this situation?
- What consequences will I have to experience?

Step 4: Decide what to do.

Find out the answers to these questions:
- What do I have to do to make the people I may have hurt feel better?
- What do I need to do to make myself feel better?

Make sure that the things you decide to do are not harmful to yourself or to others.

Step 5: Do what you have decided to do.

If you have hurt other people, you need to do what you can to make them feel better. Make sure that you
- admit that you have done something wrong,
- say that you are sorry,
- do whatever you can to make up for your wrongdoing (make sure that your efforts are acceptable to the people you have hurt), and
- try not to do the same thing again.

You also need to make yourself feel better. Make sure that you
- remember that you are a human being (you are not perfect, and it is normal for you to make mistakes),
- forgive yourself when you do something that is wrong,
- learn whatever you can from the situation, and
- try not to do the same thing again.

Step 6: Talk about your thoughts and feelings.

A tough situation can cause you to have many thoughts and feelings that should not be ignored. Pay attention to them. Share them with someone else. When you talk to someone, you need to make sure that the person is

- someone who you respect and can trust,
- someone who cares about you, and
- someone who is old enough and wise enough to help you.

Talking about a tough situation one time will probably not make everything OK. Therefore, you need to continue to talk about your thoughts and feelings for as long as you feel a need to do so.

Here are six steps for handling tough situations you did **not** create:

Step 1: Face it.

Admit that you are experiencing a tough situation. Do not pretend that everything is OK.

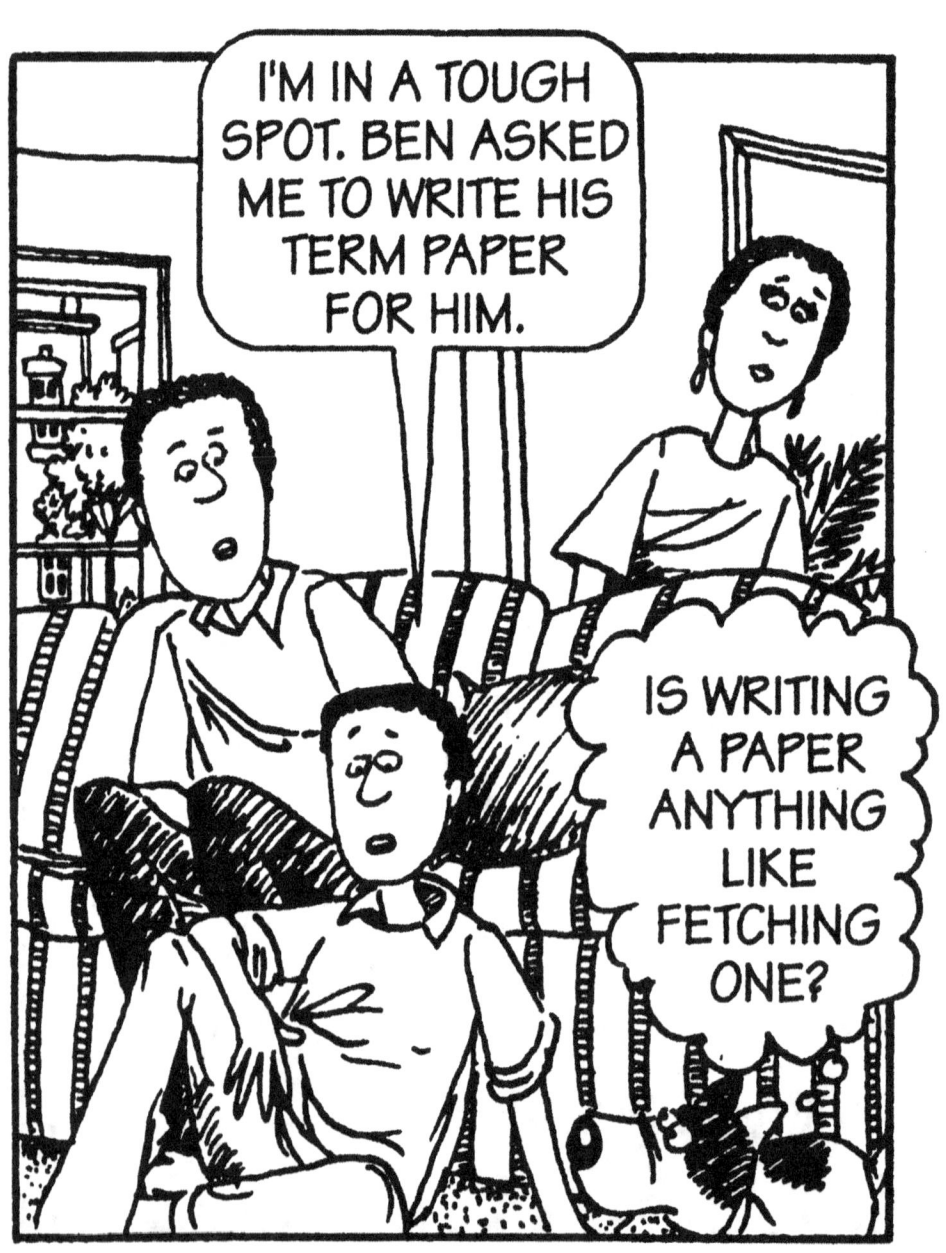

Step 2: Accept it.

Accept this fact: The tough situation is not going to go away automatically. Realize that you are going to have to put some time and effort into resolving it.

STEPS FOR HANDLING TOUGH SITUATIONS YOU DID NOT CREATE

Step 3: Think about it.

Find out the answers to these questions:
- What happened to create this tough situation?
- What is going to happen to me?

Step 4: Decide what to do.

Find out the answers to these questions:
- What can I do to make the situation better?
- What can I do to make myself feel better?
- What can I do to make the other people who are involved in this situation feel better?

Step 5: Do what you have decided to do.

If possible you should
- talk to the people who created the tough situation (if you cannot talk to them, talk to someone else),
- try to understand why these people did what they did,
- try to forgive them,
- do not blame yourself in any way, and
- do whatever you can to make yourself and the other people involved in the situation feel better.

Step 6: Talk about your thoughts and feelings.

It is important that you continue to talk over your thoughts and feelings about the tough situation until you feel better.

It will be easier to handle a tough situation if you are calm.

A good way to calm yourself is to
- stop whatever you are doing,
- take several deep breaths and let them out slowly, and
- relax your body.

Here is one way to relax your body:
- Slowly count to ten.
- Tense your entire body more and more with each count. By the time your reach 10, your body should feel completely tense from your head to your toes.
- Slowly count backwards from ten.
- Relax your entire body more and more with each count. By the time you reach 1, your body should feel completely relaxed all over.

It will be easier to handle a tough situation if you slow down your thoughts and focus them on dealing with the situation.

Avoid doing anything that will cloud your thinking.

This includes using substances such as alcohol or nonprescription drugs to calm yourself.

It will be easier to handle a tough situation if you remember these six facts:

Fact #1. There are some good things about every situation. Try not to focus on the bad things about a situation. Instead, look for the good things and focus your attention on them. This will help prevent you from becoming so depressed that you cannot deal appropriately with the situation.

Fact #2: Things could always be worse.

Try to realize that no matter how bad a situation seems to be, it could always be worse. Be thankful that it is not worse. Being thankful will help you to feel better.

Fact #3. Every problem has a solution.
When a tough situation creates problems for you, try not to waste your time and energy feeling bad about them. Instead, realize that there are solutions to your problems. Spend your time and energy finding the solutions. This will help you to overcome the problems and to feel better.

Fact #4: Every person can find the solutions to his or her problems.
Remember that every person has the ability on their own or with the help of others, to find the solutions to any problem. Realizing this will help prevent you from giving up before your problems are resolved.

Fact #5: "This too shall pass."
Remember that just as every experience has a beginning, it also has an ending. This includes any tough situation that you encounter. Realizing this can make it easier for you to endure difficult times.

Fact #6: "Time heals all wounds."
Remember, by handling tough situations in a positive way, the pain you experience most likely will fade with the passing of time. Realizing this can make it easier for you to endure difficult times.

CONCLUSION

Tough situations do not have negative endings automatically.

Tough situations can have positive endings if they are handled appropriately.

CONCLUSION

Tough situations that are handled appropriately can help you grow and to become a better person.

www.ingramcontent.com/pod-product-compliance
Lightning Source LLC
Chambersburg PA
CBHW081409070526
44583CB00020B/2735